# He Is Exalted

T0087644

Recorded and produced by Jim Reith at BeatHouse Music, Milwaukee, WI

Lead Vocals by Tonia Emrich and Jim Reith
Background Vocals by Jim Reith and Joy Palisoc Bach
Guitar by Jim Reith
Bass by Chris Kringel
Keyboard by Kurt Cowling
Drums by Del Bennett

ISBN 978-1-4234-1726-2

**HAL•LEONARD®**
CORPORATION
7777 W. BLUEMOUND RD. P.O. BOX 13819 MILWAUKEE, WI 53213

Visit Hal Leonard Online at
**www.halleonard.com**

# Beautiful One

**Words and Music by Tim Hughes**

TRACKS
1/2

With energy ( = 132)

**Intro**

**A** **Verse 1**

Won - der - ful, so ____ won - der - ful is Your un - fail - ing ____

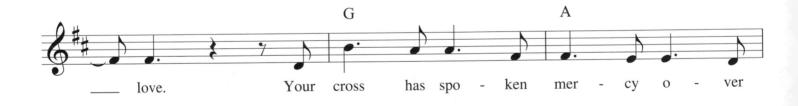

____ love. Your cross has spo - ken mer - cy o - ver

me.                No eye has seen, no ____

____ ear has heard, no heart could ____ ful - ly ____ know          how

won - der - ful You ___ are. ___                    Beau - ti - ful

**D** Chorus

One    I    love, ___    Beau - ti - ful One    I    a -

dore,    Beau - ti - ful One,    my    soul    must ___

sing. ___    Beau - ti - ful One    I    love, ___

Chorus

___    Beau - ti - ful One    I    a - dore,    Beau - ti - ful

One,    my    soul    must ___    sing. ___

**E** Bridge

___    You o - pened my eyes ___ to Your won - ders a - new, ___ You cap-

- tured my heart with this ___ love,    'cause noth - ing on earth ___ is as beau-

4

# God of All

**Words and Music by Twila Paris**

TRACKS
3/4

Moderately ( = 89)

**Intro**

E        B/D#         C#m7        Bsus

E        B/D#         C#m7        Bsus

**A** **Verse**

E        B/D#

God of all, __ we come to praise __ You. __ We

A/C#        Bsus

lift Your name __ on high __ in all the earth. __

E        B/D#

God of all, __ we come to praise __ You. __ We

A/C#        Bsus

lift Your name __ on high __ in all __ the earth. __ God of __

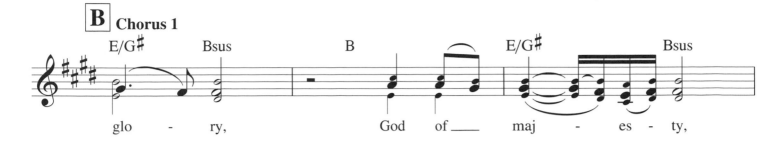

**B** **Chorus 1**

glo - ry, God of ___ maj - es - ty,

God of ___ mer - cy, we lift Your name on

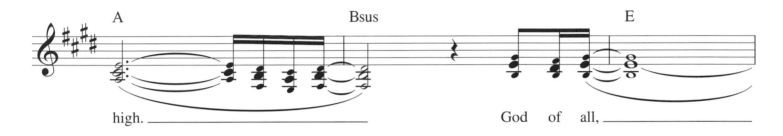

high. ___ God of all, ___

God of all. ___

**C** **Verse**

God of all, ___ we come to praise ___ You. ___ We

lift Your name ___ on high ___ in all the earth. ___

God of all, ___ we come to praise ___ You. ___ We

A/C#  Bsus

lift Your name _ on high _ in all _ the earth. _  God of _

**D** Chorus 2

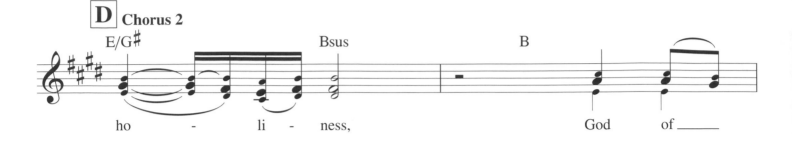

E/G#  Bsus  B

ho - li - ness,  God of _

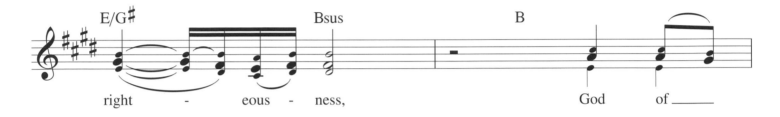

E/G#  Bsus  B

right - eous - ness,  God of _

E/G#  Bsus  E/G#  A

heav - en, we lift Your name on high. _

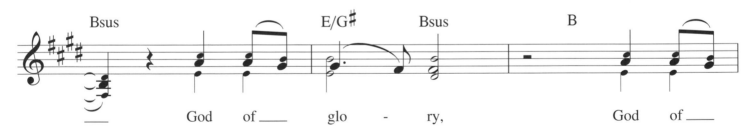

Bsus  E/G#  Bsus  B

_  God of _ glo - ry,  God of _

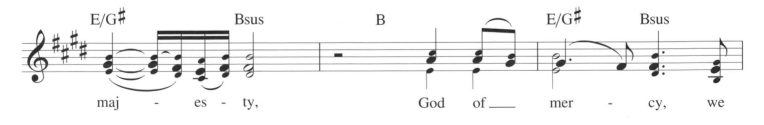

E/G#  Bsus  B  E/G#  Bsus

maj - es - ty,  God of _ mer - cy, we

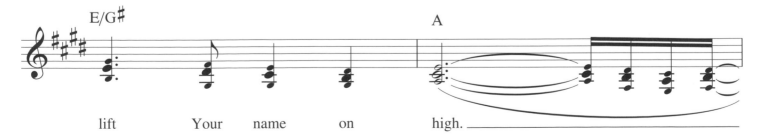

E/G#  A

lift Your name on high. _

# He Is Exalted

## Words and Music by Twila Paris

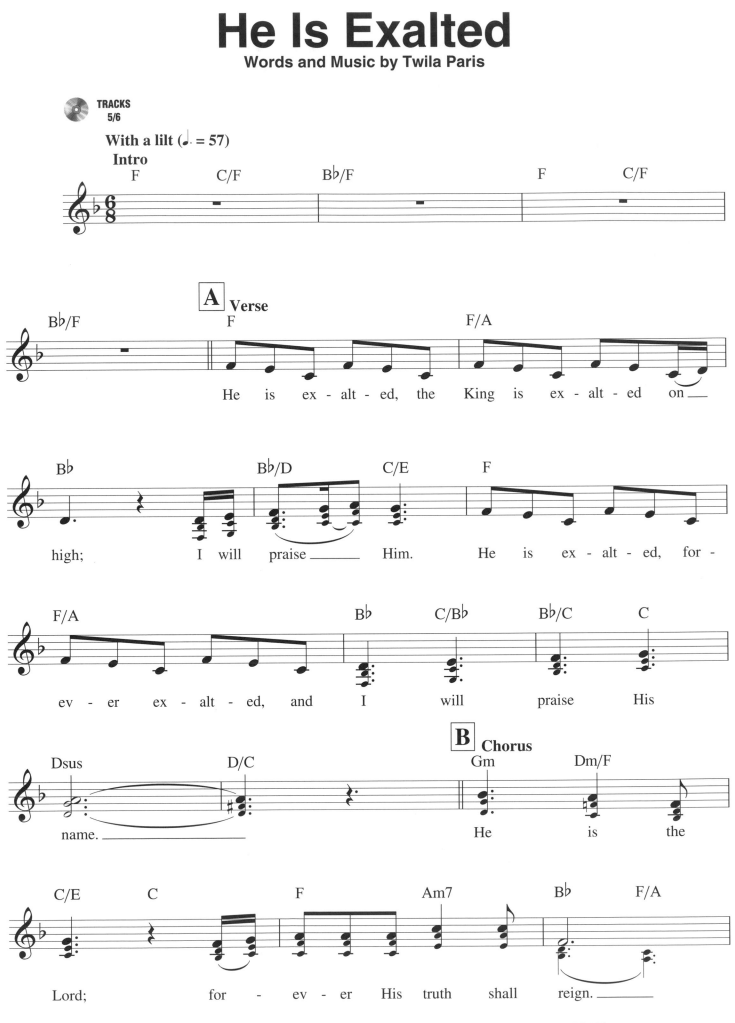

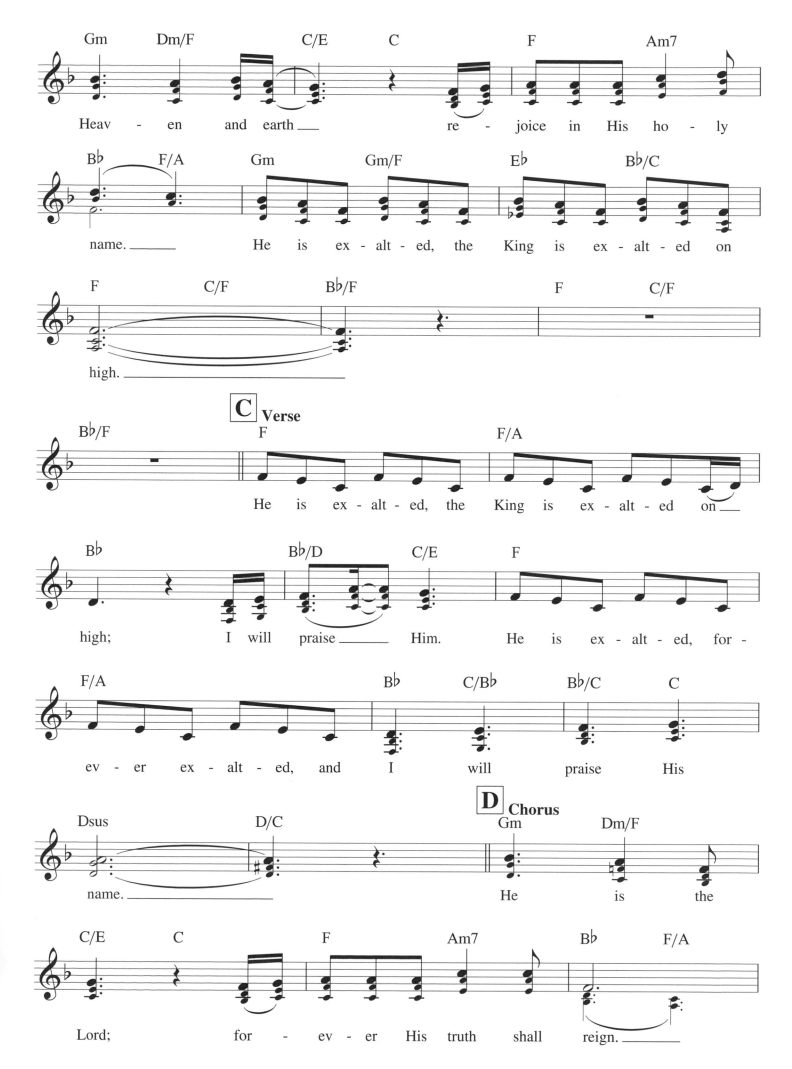

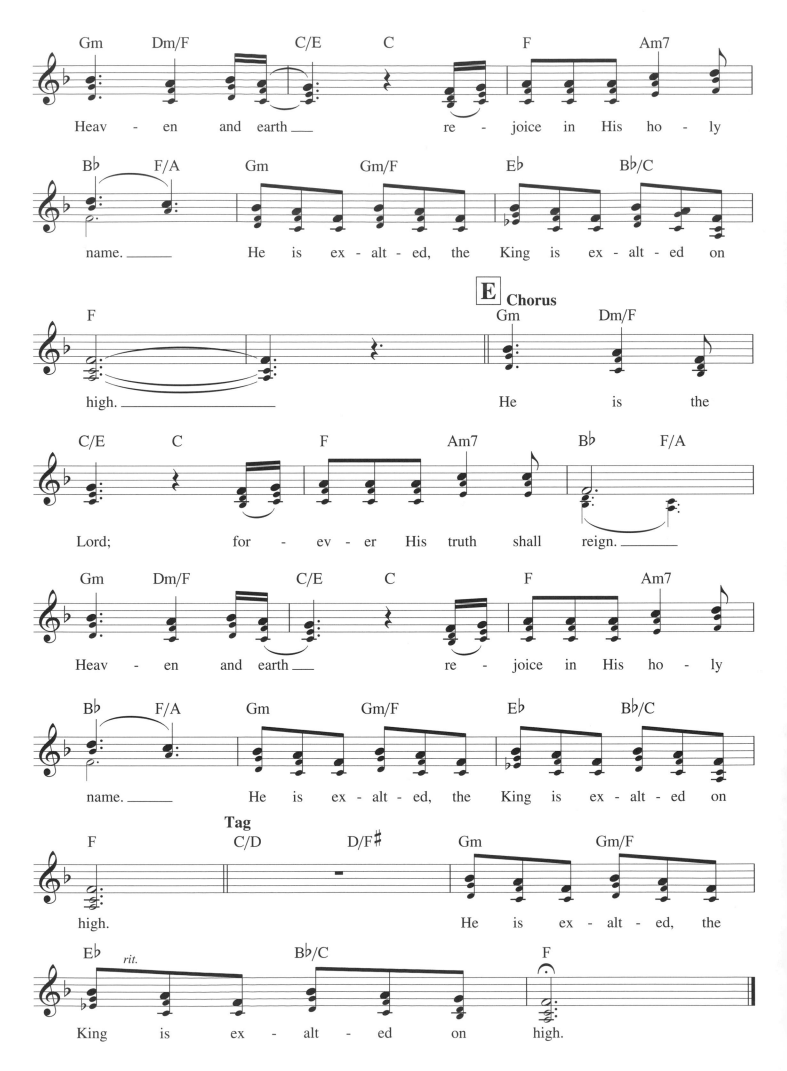

Heav - en and earth ___ re - joice in His ho - ly name. ___ He is ex - alt - ed, the King is ex - alt - ed on

**E** Chorus

high. ___ He is the Lord; for - ev - er His truth shall reign. ___ Heav - en and earth ___ re - joice in His ho - ly name. ___ He is ex - alt - ed, the King is ex - alt - ed on

**Tag**

high. ___ He is ex - alt - ed, the King is ex - alt - ed on high.

# Lord, Reign in Me

**Words and Music by Brenton Brown**

# In Christ Alone

**Words and Music by Keith Getty
and Stuart Townend**

# Lord Most High

### Words and Music by Don Harris and Gary Sadler

Bsus     B     C#m7

from the   heights   of   the   heav - ens,     (from the
depths   of   the   sea,) __

A    E/A    A

Your   name   be   praised.     From   the
heights   of   the   heav - ens, Your   name   be   praised.)

E       Esus    E

hearts   of   the   weak, _   (From   the   hearts   of   the   weak,) _ from   the

B       Bsus    B

shouts   of   the   strong, _   (from   the   shouts   of   the   strong,) _ from   the

C#m7                  A    E/A

lips   of   all   peo - ple,           this   song   we
(from   the   lips   of   all   peo - ple, this   song   we

**D** **Chorus 2**

A   B     E   E/G#       A     B     E   E/G#

raise,   Lord. )
raise,   Lord,) )    Through-out the   end - less __ ag - es, __       You will be

A       B     C#m7   A     Bsus   B     E    E/G#

crowned with _ prais - es, __   Lord   Most   High.       Ex - alt - ed   in

# We Want to See Jesus Lifted High

**Words and Music by Doug Horley**

we want to see, we want to see Je - sus lift - ed high. __ We want to see, we want to see, we want to see Je -

**F** Bridge

- sus lift - ed high. __ Step by step, we're mov - ing for - ward. Lit - tle by lit - tle, tak - ing ground. _ Ev - 'ry prayer a pow'r - ful wea - pon; strong - holds come tum - bl - ing down _

**G** Verse

__ and down _ and down __ and down. __ We want to see Je - sus lift - ed high, __ a ban - ner that flies __ a - cross _ this land, __ that all men might see __ the truth _ and know __ He is the way _

# Worthy Is the Lamb

### Words and Music by Darlene Zschech

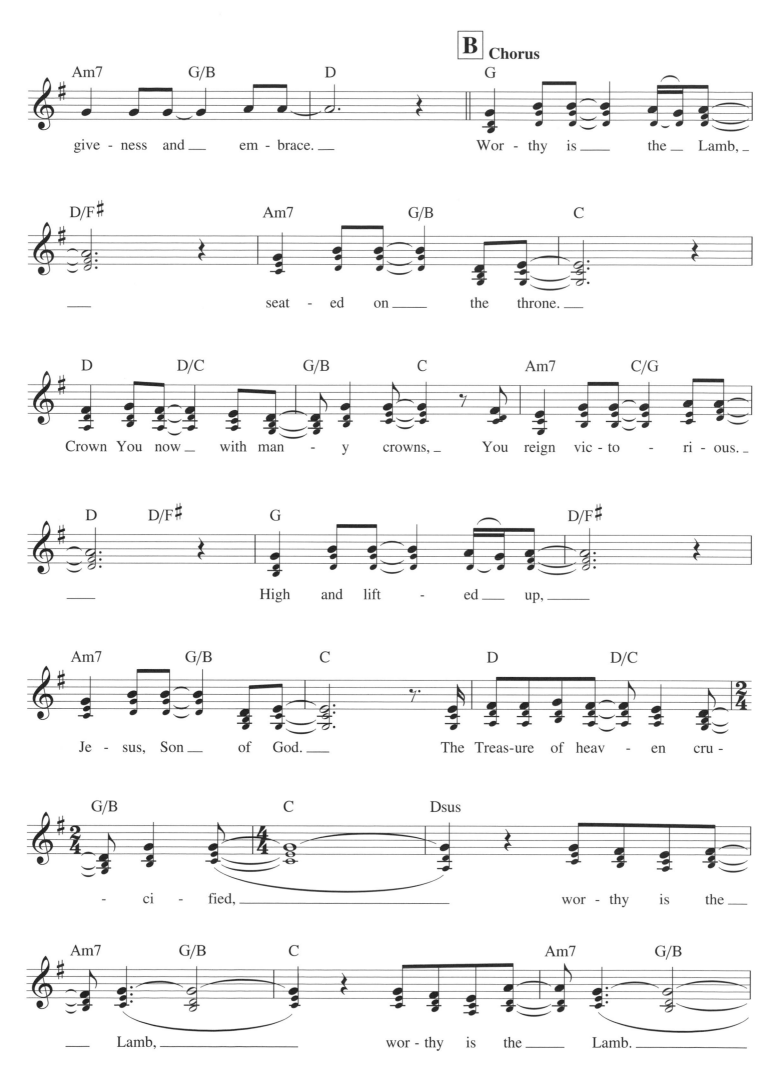

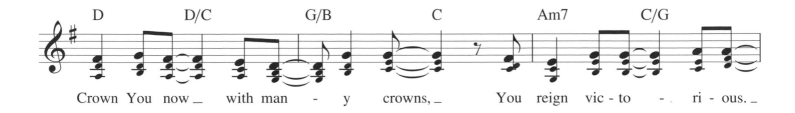

Crown You now __ with man - y crowns, __ You reign vic - to - ri - ous. __

__ High and lift - ed __ up, __

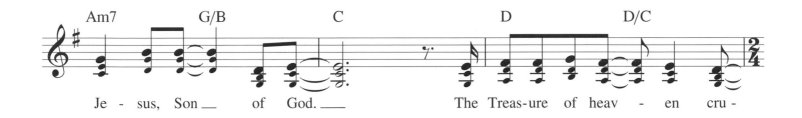

Je - sus, Son __ of God. __ The Treas-ure of heav - en cru -

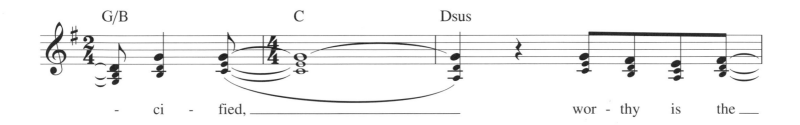

- ci - fied, _____ wor - thy is the __

__ Lamb, _____ wor - thy is the __ Lamb.

**E** **Chorus**

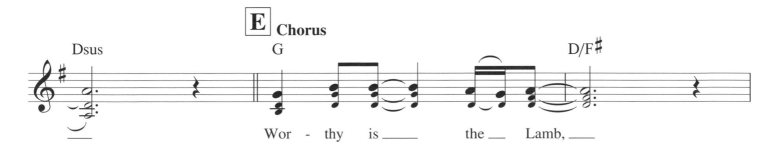

Wor - thy is __ the __ Lamb, __

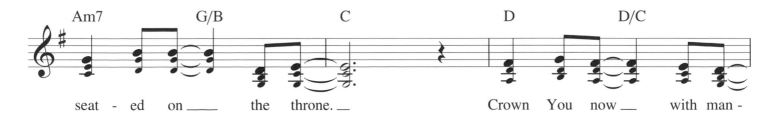

seat - ed on __ the throne. __ Crown You now __ with man -

-y crowns,___ You reign vic - to - ri - ous.____

High and lift - ed___ up, ____ Je - sus, Son___ of God.__

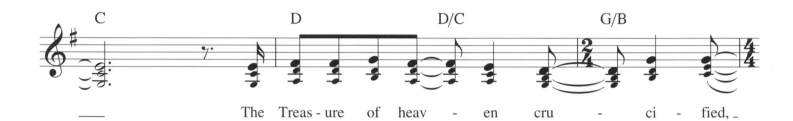

___ The Treas - ure of heav - en cru - ci - fied, _

_____ wor - thy is the _____ Lamb, _____

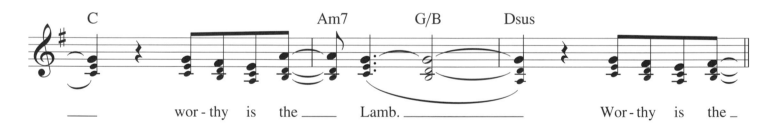

___ wor - thy is the ___ Lamb. _____ Wor - thy is the _

**F** **Tag**

___ Lamb, _____ wor - thy is the ___ Lamb. _____

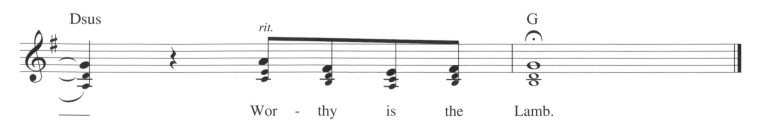

___ Wor - thy is the Lamb.

# BEAUTIFUL ONE

TIM HUGHES

Key of **D Major**, 4/4

## *INTRO:*

G  A  Bm7  A

G  A  D

## *VERSE 1:*

G           A     D/F♯
Wonderful, so wonderful is Your unfailing love

    G           A     Bm7
Your cross has spoken mercy over me

    G          A         D/F♯
No eye has seen, no ear has heard, no heart could fully know

    G       A     D
How glorious, how beautiful You are

## *CHORUS:*

       G   A     G   A
Beautiful One I love, Beautiful One I adore

       G   A     D
Beautiful One, my soul must sing

## *VERSE 2:*

G       A     D/F♯
Powerful, so powerful, Your glory fills the skies

    G       A     Bm7
Your mighty works displayed for all to see

    G     A    D/F♯
The beauty of Your majesty awakes my heart to sing:

    G      A     D
How marvelous, how wonderful You are

## *(REPEAT CHORUS 2X)*

## *BRIDGE (2X):*

    G            A
You opened my eyes to Your wonders anew

    G           A
You captured my heart with this love

    G        A     D
'Cause nothing on earth is as beautiful as You

## *(REPEAT CHORUS 2X)*

# GOD OF ALL
TWILA PARIS

Key of **E Major**, 4/4

### INTRO (2X):

E   B/D♯   C♯m7   Bsus

### VERSE:

E          B/D♯
God of all, we come to praise You

   A/C♯                 Bsus
We lift Your name on high in all the earth

E          B/D♯
God of all, we come to praise You

   A/C♯                 Bsus
We lift Your name on high in all the earth

### CHORUS 1:

     E/G♯  Bsus  B     E/G♯  Bsus  B
God of glo - ry,       God of maj - es - ty

     E/G♯  Bsus  E/G♯        A  Bsus
God of mer - cy, we lift Your name on high

       E  A  Bsus       E  A  Bsus
God of all,          God of all

### (REPEAT VERSE)

### CHORUS 2:

     E/G♯   Bsus    B     E/G♯   Bsus   B
God of ho - li - ness,      God of righteousness

     E/G♯  Bsus  E/G♯          A  Bsus
God of heav - en, we lift Your name on high

     E/G♯  Bsus  B     E/G♯  Bsus  B
God of glo - ry,       God of maj - es - ty

     E/G♯  Bsus  E/G♯        A  Bsus
God of mer - cy, we lift Your name on high

### TAG:

     E                              A      Bsus
God of all (We lift Your name on high, we lift Your name on high) **REPEAT 4X**

     E (hold)
God of all

# HE IS EXALTED

TWILA PARIS

Key of **F Major, 6/8**

### INTRO:

F  C/F  B♭/F

F  C/F  B♭/F


### VERSE:

F               F/A         B♭
He is exalted, the King is exalted on high

     B♭/D   C/E
I will praise Him

F             F/A
He is exalted, forever exalted

    B♭  C/B♭  B♭/C   C  Dsus   D/C
And I   will    praise His name


### CHORUS:

Gm  Dm/F   C/E  C
He      is the Lord

    F        Am7      B♭    F/A
Forever His truth shall reign

Gm  Dm/F    C/E  C
Heav - en and earth

    F        Am7  B♭   F/A
Rejoice in His holy name

Gm   Gm/F       E♭     B♭/C      (F)
He is exalted, the King is exalted on high


### (REPEAT INTRO)


### (REPEAT VERSE)


### (REPEAT CHORUS 2X)


### TAG:

C/D  D/F♯  Gm   Gm/F      E♭    B♭/C     F (hold)
           He is exalted, the King is exalted on high

# IN CHRIST ALONE

KEITH GETTY and STUART TOWNEND

Key of **D Major**, 3/4

### INTRO (2X):

**Am7    Em7    D   Dsus   D**

### VERSE 1:

  **G/D    D       G       A**
In Christ alone my hope is found

**D/F♯    G       Em7  Asus    D**
He is my light, my strength,    my song

  **G/D    D       G       A**
This Cornerstone, this solid ground

**D/F♯            G       Em7  Asus    D**
Firm through the fiercest drought  and storm

   **D/F♯    G       D/F♯    A**
What heights of love, what depths of peace

   **D/F♯    G       Bm7       A**
When fears are stilled when strivings cease

  **G       D       G       A**
My Comforter, my All in All

**D/F♯      G       Em7  Asus    D**
Here in the love of  Christ      I stand

**(Dsus  D)**

### VERSE 2:

In Christ alone, who took on flesh
Fullness of God in helpless Babe
This gift of love and righteousness
Scorned by the ones He came to save
'Til on that cross as Jesus died
The wrath of God was satisfied
For ev'ry sin on Him was laid
Here in the death of Christ I live

### INTERLUDE:

**Am7    Em7    D   Dsus   D**

### VERSE 3:

There in the ground His body lay
Light of the world by darkness slain
Then bursting forth in glorious day
Up from the grave He rose again!
And as He stands in victory
Sin's curse has lost its grip on me
For I am His and He is mine
Bought with the precious blood of Christ

**(Dsus  D)**

### VERSE 4:

No guilt in life, no fear in death
This is the pow'r of Christ in me
From life's first cry to final breath
Jesus commands my destiny
No pow'r of hell, no scheme of man
Can ever pluck me from His hand
'Til He returns or calls me home
Here in the pow'r of Christ I'll stand

### TAG:

   **D/F♯      G       D/F♯      A**
No pow'r of hell, no scheme of man

   **D/F♯    G       Bm7       A**
Can ever pluck me from His hand

  **G       D       G       A**
'Til He returns or calls me home

**D/F♯            G       Em7  Asus      D**
Here in the pow'r of Christ       I'll stand

**D/F♯            G       Em7  Asus      D (hold)**
Here in the pow'r of Christ       I'll stand

# LORD MOST HIGH

DON HARRIS and GARY SADLER

Key of **E Major**, 6/8

**INTRO (2X):**

E   Esus   E   Esus2

**VERSE:**

          E              *Echo:*    Esus      E
From the ends of the earth (from the ends of the earth)
        B                   Bsus    B
From the depths of the sea (from the depths of the sea)
     C♯m7
From the heights of the heavens (from the heights of the heavens)
    A  E/A  A
Your name be praised
         E                   Esus      E
From the hearts of the weak (from the hearts of the weak)
        B                   Bsus    B
From the shouts of the strong (from the shouts of the strong)
     C♯m7
From the lips of all people (from the lips of all people)
    A  E/A  A    B
This song we raise, Lord

**CHORUS 1:**

E  E/G♯         A     B
Throughout the endless ages
E  E/G♯    A        B
You will be crowned with praises
C♯m7  A  Bsus  B
Lord Most High
E   E/G♯   A     B
Exalted in ev'ry nation
E  E/G♯     A      B
Sov'reign of all creation
C♯m7  A   B  E/G♯     A
Lord Most High, be magnified

**(REPEAT VERSE)**

**CHORUS 2:**

E  E/G♯         A     B
Throughout the endless ages
E  E/G♯    A        B
You will be crowned with praises
C♯m7  A  Bsus  B
Lord Most High
E   E/G♯   A     B
Exalted in ev'ry nation
E  E/G♯     A      B
Sov'reign of all creation
C♯m7  A  Bsus  B
Lord Most High

**(REPEAT CHORUS 1)**

**TAG:**

B              E  E/G♯  A
        Be magnified          **REPEAT 2X**
B        E (hold)
Be magnified

# LORD, REIGN IN ME

BRENTON BROWN

Key of **G Major**, 4/4

### INTRO:

G D C  G D C

### VERSE 1:

```
G         D       C          D
   Over all the earth, You reign on high
G         D        C           D
   Ev'ry mountain stream, ev'ry sunset sky
Em7       D       C         D    Am7
   But my one request, Lord, my only aim
              C     D
Is that You'd reign in me again
```

### CHORUS:

```
G          D       C        D
   Lord, reign in me, reign in Your pow'r
G          D        C          D
   Over all my dreams, in my darkest hour
Em7      D       C    D    Am7
   You are the Lord of all I am
            C     D
So won't You reign in me again?
```

### INTERLUDE:

G D C  G D C

### VERSE 2:

```
G          D         C            D
   Over ev'ry thought, over ev'ry word
G           D      C               D
   May my life reflect the beauty of my Lord
Em7              D    C          D    Am7
   'Cause You mean more to me than any earthly thing
              C     D
So won't You reign in me again?
```

### (REPEAT CHORUS 3X)

### TAG:

```
Am7            C      D
   Won't You reign in me again?
```

### OUTRO:

G D C  G D C (hold)

# WE WANT TO SEE JESUS LIFTED HIGH

DOUG HORLEY

Key of **G Major**, 4/4

**INTRO (2X):**

G  D   Em  C

**VERSE:**

G                    D
   We want to see Jesus lifted high
Em              C
   A banner that flies across this land
G                    D
   That all men might see the truth and know
Em          C
   He is the way to heaven

**(REPEAT VERSE)**

**CHORUS 1:**

G                    D
  We want to see,   we want to see
Em                C  G/B  Am7    G
  We want to see Je - sus     lift - ed high
G                    D
  We want to see,   we want to see
Em                C  G/B  Am7    G
  We want to see Je - sus     lift - ed high

**INTERLUDE:**

G  D   Em  C

**(REPEAT VERSE & CHORUS 1)**

**BRIDGE:**

       D                        Em
Step by step, we're moving forward
       D                  Em
Little by little, taking ground
       D                    Em
Ev'ry prayer a pow'rful weapon
          C                    D
Strongholds come tumbling down
   and down and down and down

**(REPEAT VERSE & CHORUS 1)**

**CHORUS 2:**

G                    D
  We're gonna see,   we're gonna see
Em                C  G/B  Am7    G
  We're gonna see Je - sus     lift - ed high
G                    D
  We're gonna see,   we're gonna see
Em                C  G/B  Am7    G
  We're gonna see Je - sus     lift - ed high

**OUTRO:** *(Vocal ad lib.)*

G  D   Em  C

G  D   Em  C  G/B  Am7  G

# WORTHY IS THE LAMB

DARLENE ZSCHECH

Key of **G Major**, 4/4

**INTRO:**

Em7   G   Em7   G

**VERSE:**

              C        G/B
Thank You for the cross, Lord

             C    D   G
Thank You for the price You paid

           D/E    Em7      D      C
Bearing all my sin and shame, in love You came

  Am7   G/B    D
And gave amazing grace

G       G/B     C       G/B
Thank You for this love, Lord

           C   D      G
Thank You for the nail-pierced hands

           D/E    Em7     D   C
Washed me in Your cleansing flow, now all I know:

  Am7     G/B    D
Your forgiveness and embrace

**CHORUS:**

G           D/F♯  Am7  G/B   C
Worthy is the Lamb, seated on the throne

D      D/C    G/B  C      Am7  C/G   D   D/F♯
Crown You now with many crowns, You reign victorious

G           D/F♯  Am7  G/B   C
High and lifted up,   Jesus, Son of God

     D         D/C   G/B  C   Dsus
The Treasure of heaven crucified

     Am7   G/B   C
Worthy is the Lamb

     Am7   G/B   Dsus
Worthy is the Lamb

**(REPEAT VERSE)**

**(REPEAT CHORUS 2X)**

**TAG:**

               Am7  G/B  C
Worthy is the Lamb

               Am7  G/B  Dsus
Worthy is the Lamb

            G (hold)
Worthy is the Lamb